M000093596

WRITERS REPUBLIC

Listen...
God Speaks Hope!

A Collection of Divine Thoughts and Prayers for Life's Journey

Rita,

Walk in God's Hope!

L. Castain

REV. DR. LORRAINE RUFF CASTAIN

WRITERS REPUBLIC L.L.C.
515 Summit Ave. Unit R1
Union City, NJ 07087, USA

Website: *www.writersrepublic.com*
Hotline: *1-877-656-6838*
Email: *info@writersrepublic.com*

Ordering Information:
Quantity sales. Special discounts are available on quantity purchases by corporations, associations, and others. For details, contact the publisher at the address above.

Library of Congress Control Number: 2021908991
ISBN-13:   978-1-63728-353-0   [Paperback Edition]
                        978-1-63728-383-7   [Hardback Edition]
                        978-1-63728-354-7   [Digital Edition]

Rev. date: 05/18/2021

Dedication

This book is dedicated to God and All of His Wondrous Works!

I also dedicate this book to the memory of my dear parents, Winslow H. and Marie C. Ruff. Without them and their dedication to raising me as best they knew how, I would not be the person I am today! Their love and example of living a life of hospitality and service to God are the tools they instilled in me. Because of their gentle care through the years, I can face the challenges of life and thrive through every storm while always giving God praise!

To God be the glory for He continues to do great things for me!

Reflections

When God speaks, there will always be a message of hope in God's words. God told the ancient prophet Jeremiah, "I know the plans I have for you...plans for your welfare and not your harm - to give you a future with hope" (Jer. 29:11). Rev. Dr. Lorraine Castain is a witness of God's message of hope. In her preaching, teaching, and care, she exudes the hope that comes from God. Now, she reflects that hope in her ministry of writing. In the pages that follow, Dr. Castain will testify how God has held her in tough times, good times, and common times through God's message of hope. She will reflect on her life's journey and impress upon every reader how she was filled with hope after having life transforming encounters with God. Dr. Castain won't just share sound precepts and responsible theology; she will share her heart and her life. Please read these pages with an open mind and spirit. Allow her words to touch you and see what transpires. I suspect that you will walk away with an expectation - an expectation that God's promises over your life will come true. That, my friend, is hope!

Dr. Castain is a proud member of Bethel African Methodist Episcopal Church in Baltimore, MD. I have the honor of serving as the Senior Pastor. It has been my joy to know Dr. Castain the past few years, and all of us at Bethel are so proud of her and her ministry.

Dr. Castain - Bethel celebrates you and all that God is doing in you. You are a testament that when God speaks, hope is sure to follow. May God bless every person who reads your work to encounter a Divine hope that will anchor them in the midst of life's difficulties. May God also bless you Dr. Castain to continue growing as an author, minister, preacher, prophet, teacher, evangelist, caregiver, and disciple of Jesus.

Listen! God speaks hope!!!

Rev. Patrick D. Clayborn, Ph.D.
Senior Pastor
Bethel African Methodist Episcopal Church

Listen...

The Father's Covering

Scripture:

Genesis 12:1-3 (NRSV)

1 Now the Lord said to Abram, "Go from your country and your kindred and your father's house to the land that I will show you.
2 I will make of you a great nation, and I will bless you, and make your name great, so that you will be a blessing.
3 I will bless those who bless you, and the one who curses you I will curse; and in you all the families of the earth shall be blessed."

Message of Hope:

My father passed away in August 1979, yet there are times when it seems like it was just yesterday when God called him to his heavenly home. No one ever fully recovers from the loss of a loved one. Whether the memories are happy or hurtful, the loss lingers in the heart. There are always those special times of year...Thanksgiving, Christmas, Valentine's Day and Father's Day when I miss my father most. I grieved his death for several years. The grace that carried me through my grief was the realization that I still and always will have a Heavenly Father.

In Genesis 12:1-3, Abram is called away, by God, to leave his father and all of the comforts of living with his father and family. Scripture does not mention that Abram was aware of where God was leading him. There is also no mention of any hesitation in Abram's willingness to leave his father. Genesis 12:4 tells us "So Abram went as the Lord told him;...." There's also no mention of Abram enduring the grief of being separated from his father. Whenever God instructed him to move, Abram moved as an act of faith and great regard for God as his Heavenly Father. God kept His covenant with Abram and was faithful to bless and protect Abram along his life's journey.

During the many experiences of loss and separation from the people and things we hold dear to our hearts, we can find great comfort in knowing we share in the relationship with our Heavenly Father! He gives us brand new life every morning and protects us along life's journey! Our Father is a provider who will keep His promises to us as He did with Abram.

If you have ever been separated from a loved one by death or other circumstances, be assured that you were not left alone. Whatever the situation, we have a Heavenly Father who knows all about our struggles! This Father is only a deep breath, thought, prayer, or praise away!

When special memories of my father visit my heart, they are now met with joy instead of sadness. As I believe my father's spirit and teachings are still with me to guide me, I also know my Heavenly Father faithfully watches over me. This message honors my earthly father and recognizes the awesome wonder of The Almighty Father!

Prayer:

Thank You, God, for being my Father! Your love and Your caring ways are like no other! You cover me, protect me, and provide for me! Loved ones may pass away, but You will always be with me! It is with thanksgiving and by the Mighty Name of Your Son, Jesus, I pray! Amen!

Think About It:

I trust in God wherever I may be,
Upon the land or on the rolling sea,
For come what may, from day to day,
Tho billows roll He keeps my soul
My Heavenly Father watches over me!

(*My Father Watches Over Me*, William C. Martin - 1910)

Listen...

A Mid-Week Morning Prayer

Good Morning, Father!

Thank You for Your mercy and grace that brings me to the middle of the week!

I have arrived here because of Your love, provision, and protection.

Father, please continue to carry the sorrow of those who grieve.

Lord, please cover the streets of all of the cities and towns of this nation.

Lord, I praise You for the day when minds are healed and hearts are mended.

I give You glory, in advance, for a world where respect and honesty are commonplace.

Regardless of the condition of society, I know You are in control.

When my heart is overwhelmed, I know I can draw close to You for comfort and peace.

In You, there is a blessed assurance of a Father who knows all, hears our prayers, and sees our tears.

I do love You and look to You for all things!

As I press towards the end of this week, I pray that my voice, my smile and my attitude shows some lost soul that all of creation belongs to You.

Humbling my spirit and lifting my eyes to You, I know I can go on by Your grace.

In the Precious Name of Your Son, Jesus, and by His example, I trust and pray! Amen!

Listen...

A Prayer for When We Don't Know What to Say

When everything around us seems crazy and we don't know what to think or say, it's time to pray!

Father, I praise and bless Your Holy Name!
You remain on the throne and I remain a part of Your creation!
There is no wavering of who You are and no question of Your mighty power. In all that You are, I look to You!

Father, you know the depth of the turmoil in this world. Tragedies, homelessness, hatred and all forms of evil have become commonplace among humanity.

Mass shootings, issues of addiction and abuse, racism and political disputes are a routine part of our daily local and national news reports.

Yet, my heart is comforted to know there is a power higher than anything this world can imagine. There is a great and divine Decision Maker who has the final say.

Your Word tells us to humble ourselves and pray and move from our wicked ways and You will heal our land! Father, I am here...humbling myself and turning to You for myself as I also plead for others.

Please cover the earth with Your glory.
Please heal and deliver us from all evil.

You alone are God and You alone can do this.
I lean on, trust, and place my hope in You.
I reach out to You for every wounded soul and every broken heart.
Within my spirit, I imagine and hope for a peaceful and safe world for all!

In the Name of Your Son, Jesus, I pray as I humbly give all glory and honor to You! Amen!

Listen...

A Prayer When You are In the Middle

Most Righteous Father, I honor and praise You for the power of Your Mighty Name!

As I arise today, my heart pleads for those who stand in the middle. Some of us are in the middle of life changing decisions while others are simply in the middle of life's journey.

We stand in the middle of turmoil running rampant across the nation. This nation barely manages to make it through the middle of its daily challenges. At the end of the day, many souls are weary and wounded. I pray for those who are standing in the middle of sickness, grief, and despair.

Thank You God for Your Son Jesus who stood in the middle of sin for us more than 2,000 years ago!

Because of Your love, through Jesus, we can survive the middle!

God I pray that my actions and words please You today. Please forgive me if I try to take short cuts to get out of the middle before it's time. Help me to shine the light of hope and be the salt this earth so desperately needs.

My heart is grateful for the middle because You are right there with me. The middle is the halfway point to my divine destiny!

So, I move forward in the middle knowing You are in control. Only You know what lies ahead, Lord, only You! In the Strong Name of Jesus, I press onward as I pray! Amen!

Listen...

Cry Out to Me!

Scripture:

Exodus 2:23-25 (NRSV)

23 After a long time the king of Egypt died. The Israelites groaned under their slavery, and cried out. Out of the slavery their cry for help rose up to God.
24 God heard their groaning, and God remembered his covenant with Abraham, Isaac, and Jacob.
25 God looked upon the Israelites, and God took notice of them.

Message of Hope:

Have you ever had a burden so heavy that it became extremely demanding of your mind, body, spirit, and emotions? Some burdens weigh on us to such a great degree that we long for someone to talk to...a shoulder to cry on. Sometimes a good cry releases all of the stress attached to our burdens.

When the troubles of life become a heavy burden and you long for someone to listen and comfort you, be sure to cry out to God first. Friends and family may listen, but they really cannot fix your problem. They will also soon grow weary of hearing about your pitiful situation. After all, they probably have their own challenges that they believe far outweighs your issues. The Lord never grows weary of our cries unto Him! He is available 24/7, 365 days!

Does crying out to God really work? Well, God heard the cries of the Israelites time after time! He heard their "groaning, and God remembered his covenant with Abraham, Isaac, and Jacob." "God looked upon the Israelites, and God took notice of them." God also heard the cries of Job and restored to him seven times more than what he lost! Moses cried out to God every time the Israelites became a challenge to lead and God gave him detailed instructions! Jesus cried out to the Father many times during His ministry on earth, to include His time on the cross, and God gave him direction, grace, strength and resurrection!

I'm not saying we should live each day in tears or walk around with a constant complaining spirit. There will be times, however, when your tears will bring healing and God's next-step directions will be made clear! Consider your tears to be a way of cleansing your mind and heart of your heavy burdens. I once heard a preacher challenge the congregation to imagine God collects all of our tears in a bucket. At the right time, God will turn that bucket upside down and our tears will be transformed into showers of blessings! From now on, think of your tears as your thanksgiving offering to God for His goodness, mercy and grace!

Prayer:

God, I am so grateful to You for always hearing my heart's cry! Help me to always turn to you first when life gets crazy! I pray, in the Strong Name of Jesus, that my faith and belief may increase daily! Amen!

Think About It:

God will take notice of me and hear my cries!
God alone can sustain me and deliver me from all trials!
God alone can change my cries of despair into praises of thanksgiving!
God and God alone!

Listen...

Every Good and Perfect Gift

Scripture:

James 1:17 (NRSV)

Every generous act of giving, with every perfect gift, is from above, coming down from the Father of lights, with whom there is no variation or shadow due to change.

Message of Hope:

Through the years, I have witnessed God pour out His blessings upon so many people, myself included. There are, however, some who don't consider cars, homes, clothing, financial security, and new job opportunities as gifts from God. There are some people who believe asking God for material things is insane.

The deeper your relationship with God becomes, the more you will understand that every spiritual gift, material blessing and personal gain is given to us by God. We achieve nothing solely on our own. Whatever we amass is provided by God's decision to bless us in such a way. You see, God is the maker of all things and He alone judges all people. Therefore, all we have and all we hope to achieve originate with God.

God's word guarantees He knows our needs. We don't have to wait to get to heaven to enjoy the goodness of God. His blessings are like showers of light falling down on us from above. If we are faithful in prayer, praise and worship, God will bless us with the desires of our hearts according to His will. When we seek a deep relationship with Him, God will openly reward our faith.

Every time you receive something new in your life, you can be assured that the blessing is a part of God's plan. So, enjoy the blessings and celebrate God with thanksgiving! Let all of His divine gifts strengthen your faith, humble your heart, and deepen your diligence in holy service.

Prayer:

Father, I thank You for all of the marvelous things You have showered upon my life! I place my relationship with You above everything! Life without You would have no meaning or purpose. Thank You for choosing to love me. You are my strength, my joy and the Giver of all things! It is with the utmost gratitude and through the Name of Your Chosen Sacrifice, Jesus, I pray! Amen!

Think About It:

Seek ye first, the kingdom of His love
Make Him first in everything you do
If you'll just trust and never doubt what He said
All good things will be added unto you!

(*All Good Things Will Be Added Unto You* - By Shelton Becton)

Listen...

Happy Birthday!

Scripture:

Psalm 139:1-2 (NRSV)

1 O Lord, you have searched me and known me.
2 You know when I sit down and when I rise up; you discern my thoughts from far away.

Message of Hope:

This is a very personal message that I hope will be a blessing to someone who needs a gentle reminder of God's love.

While on a business trip many years ago, I met another female believer during the flight. Conversation began after I noticed she was reading the Bible. As we traveled through the air, we exchanged life experiences and circumstances. We also reviewed God's Word and how it could be applied as answers to our situations.

When this sister in Christ temporarily left her seat, I glanced out the window and could hear God say to my spirit "Happy Birthday!" You see, God made (as always) the right birthday gift for me...fellowship with another believer!

As the years go by, I realize more and more that God knows me and always knows exactly what I need! I understand, to a greater degree, the promise in Philippians 4:19 - "my God will fully satisfy every need of yours according to his riches in glory in Christ Jesus." On that particular birthday, I thought I was missing out on a birthday celebration I would have preferred to enjoy at home. God knew exactly what I needed...His personal birthday message through conversation with a believer!

Prayer:

God, Thank You for knowing me so well! You know my desires before I can articulate them! You know my sorrows before the first tear falls! Truly, You are an awesome and all-knowing God who gives us exactly what we need when we need it! I love You and thank You through the Name of Your Precious Son, Jesus! Amen!

Think About It:

We are never truly alone.
God sees us and knows our needs and desires!
He will supply every need in ways that only God can provide!

Listen...

He Knows How Much You Can Bear

Scripture:

Psalm 55:22 (NRSV)

Cast your burden on the Lord, and He will sustain you; He will never permit the righteous to be moved.

Message of Hope:

As a child, my parents would try to refrain from complaining about life's struggles. I remember their favorite saying was "Things could always be worse. There's no use in complaining." Perhaps my parents knew they could handle the burdens when they turned everything over to God!

As an adult, there are times when I may not deal with difficulties as well as I should. Life is much easier to deal with when we learn to release all of our cares to God as if releasing a heavy weight. We can also find courage for ourselves when we take the time to listen to a friend or loved one and hear the hidden pain in their voice and see anguish in their actions. It is then, you will begin to realize all of us have struggles at some time or another and the struggle is more doable when we lean on The Father.

God is able to sustain us and carry us through every trial. We may fall during the challenge, but He will be there to pick us up and give us another chance. He knows how much we can bear and He knows the struggle will not utterly destroy us because He will not allow it.

When trials and disappointments exercise leverage to pull your mind and Spirit into gloom and despair, remember those words, "things could always be worse." Thank God we have a Heavenly Father who knows our capacity to bear our challenges. He also knows the lessons we need to learn. After dealing with a few of my own challenges, I know from experience that God will not give you more than you can bear. He knows you and He knows He can trust you with every challenge!

Prayer:

Father, Thank You for always watching over me! Even when my spirit is too weak to see or feel your presence, You are with me! Thank You for showing me that I only have what it takes because You are holding me up! In the Precious Name of Jesus, I pray! Amen!

Think About It:

We have the faith of this assurance
The Heavenly Father will always answer prayer
And He knows, yes He knows just how much we can bear!

(*He Knows Just How Much You Can Bear*, Roberta Martin - The New National Baptist Hymnal, 21 Century Edition, Hymn 537)

Listen...

In the Midst of It All

Scripture:

Daniel 3:28-30 (NRSV)

28 Nebuchadnezzar said, "Blessed be the God of Shadrach, Meshach, and Abednego, who has sent his angel and delivered his servants who trusted in him. They disobeyed the king's command and yielded up their bodies rather than serve and worship any god except their own God.
29 Therefore I make a decree: Any people, nation, or language that utters blasphemy against the God of Shadrach, Meshach, and Abednego shall be torn limb from limb, and their houses laid in ruins; for there is no other god who is able to deliver in this way."
30 Then the king promoted Shadrach, Meshach, and Abednego in the province of Babylon.

Message of Hope:

Shadrach, Meshach and Abednego fell upon a trying time when they refused to worship King Nebuchadnezzar. They were thrown in a fiery furnace because they would not dishonor their God! They believed God would deliver them from any plot to destroy them. In the midst of the fire, an angel of the Lord walked around with them in the furnace. The word of God says Nebuchadnezzar noticed the fourth person in the fire resembled the Son of God!

In times of doubt and seasons of stress, remembering what God has already done for me helps me to carry on. Every new challenge will seem more difficult than the one before, but God knows the end before the beginning of our challenges. He is in the middle of our storms and He is ready and able to deliver us at the right time.

Stormy times are a challenge, but the fact that you are still here is evidence that God is in the midst of it all. The only way to get to the other side of a thing is to stay on the journey to the end.

I know firsthand that struggles are real and uncomfortable. However, I must say that every struggle has strengthened me and brought me closer to God. You will pray harder and worship more sincerely when you are going through something or you will turn away from God. Let me encourage you to stay close to Him. Don't turn away! Trust me... you will need Him to lean on and to walk you through every valley experience. God will take that tough situation, devastating defeat, and heartbreaking reality and use it and you for His glory!

If you have ever seen someone glowing, smiling, laughing, serving God through their hardest struggle, you can be assured God is in the middle of their season of conflict. Once you've had your pity party, and we may have many, settle in and allow God to carry you through the storm. Family, friends, and your sweetheart may be a great source of support, but they cannot bear you up the way God can! These things we go through will not destroy us if we hold onto our faith!

Prayer:

Thank You God for always being in the middle! Thank You for covering me and caring for me when I'm too weak to care for myself! I may not always see You or feel You nearby but past experiences prove that You are always in the midst of it all! It is in the Strong Name of Your Son, Jesus, I trust, believe, and pray! Amen!

Think About It:

I've come through many hard trials
Through temptations on every hand
But it's because He loves me so dearly
He was there to answer my call
He was there always to protect me
For He's kept me in the midst of it all

(*In the Midst of It All* - by Yolanda Adams)

Listen...

In the Waiting Room

Scripture:

Isaiah 40:31 (NRSV)

...but those who wait for the Lord shall renew their strength, they shall mount up with wings like eagles, they shall run and not be weary, they shall walk and not faint.

Psalm 27:14 (NRSV)

Wait for the Lord;
Be strong, and let your heart take courage;
Wait for the Lord!

Message of Hope:

Have you ever had the challenging experience of sitting in a hospital waiting room to hear the condition of a loved one? The experience is one that is difficult to describe. Nerves are on edge as you pray and hope for the best, possibly against all odds.

The experience could resemble that of being in the Lord's waiting room. Any waiting room experience is a time of uncertainty and wonder of what stands on the other side of the wait. In the waiting season, doubts and concerns about the Lord's answer can arise. You may begin to doubt if the Lord will ever come see about you and heal the diseased places in your life. Even friends and family members may begin to question your situation, as they did with Job. In Job 2:9-10, Job's wife doubts the waiting process when she says "Do you still persist in your integrity?

Curse God and die." But he said to her "You speak as any foolish woman would speak. Shall we receive the good at the hand of God, and not receive the bad?" In all this Job did not sin with his lips."

Waiting can sometimes be misunderstood as a "do nothing" state of being. But, waiting demands many things from us. When we have decided to wait on the Lord, we must exercise patience, trust and faith in God, hope, positive thinking, and endurance. We have to draw on God's strength regardless of how dire the circumstances. Doubt will surely try to beat us up as we wait. Waiting can be exhausting as we begin to feel drained of emotions and the ability to function as usual.

When it seems you have been waiting forever, remember what the Word of God tells us about the wait. In Psalm 27:14, we are encouraged to "Wait for the Lord: be strong, and let your heart take courage; wait for the Lord!" Psalm 37:5 instructs us to "Commit your way to the Lord; trust in him; and he will act." There are divine benefits in waiting! Psalm 37:34 gives the assurance "Wait for the Lord, and keep to his way, and he will exalt you to inherit the land; you will look on the destruction of the wicked."

Sometimes, your situation may get worse before it gets better. I have had seasons of waiting that seemed to linger on and on! If this ever happens to you, remember the Lord will not allow you to totally slip. Beloved, when it seems all hope is lost and the situation lands you in the Lord's waiting room where criticism and doubts arise...keep waiting. When someone asks "Why don't you give up?"...keep waiting. When those outside your waiting room don't understand, simply respond "I'm waiting on the Lord!"

Prayer:

God, as I wait, I will also pray! While I wait, I will follow Your guidance and Your will! Leaning on Your strength, grace, and mercy, I will trust that better is on the other side of the wait! This I pray, in the Strong Name of Your Son, Jesus! Amen!

Think About It:

I don't mind waiting on the Lord!
There's new grace and strength in the waiting!
I will see His power and deliverance in the waiting!
I will wait on the Lord!

Listen...

It Has Been a Long Night

Scripture:

Psalm 30:4-5 (NRSV)

4 Sing praises to the Lord, O you his faithful ones, and give thanks to his holy name.
5 For His anger is but for a moment; his favor is for a lifetime. Weeping may endure for the night, but joy comes with the morning.

Lamentations 3:22-23 (NRSV)

22 The steadfast love of the Lord never ceases, his mercies never come to an end;
23 they are new every morning; great is your faithfulness.

Message of Hope:

David wrote Psalm 30 as a point of thanksgiving after God brought him through a night season of severe illness.

Sometimes, the night seasons in life may continue for a long time. There will be times when it seems as if morning will never come. But, I promise you the light of day will rise up to wipe away your tears, doubts and fears! How do I know this? My personal experiences and the laws of nature have shown me evidence a new day is always waiting to arise. Morning always comes after the night!

No doubt, the night seasons can be scary and uncertain. But, we don't have to wander around in the dark season without hope and peace. When you surrender to the Almighty and honestly share your doubts and scary moments with Him, God will calm your Spirit and take your hand! He will be with you on the journey to daybreak!

The grace of God sustains us through the night seasons. We can praise and serve God in our darkest of times because His new mercies are waiting to greet us in the morning! There is no way of knowing how long the night will be, but trouble doesn't have long staying power! It cannot last!

Prayer:

Father, Thank You for leading me through my dark places into Your marvelous light! When I can't see the path, I pray that I trust You as my compass. When doubts arise, I pray for bold confidence in the power of Your word. Even when it seems I'm in a midnight situation, I know I can praise You for the morning that's on the way! In the Strong Name of Jesus, the light of the world, I pray! Amen!

Think About It:

When the night is dark and you cannot find your way,
When your days are dreary and the tears will not cease to fall,
remember, the morning always follows the night!
When the sun rises, you will also rise with new grace,
new mercies and a testimony!
HALLELUJAH!! Good Morning!!!

Listen...

Never Forget!

Scripture:

Deuteronomy 8:2. (NRSV)

Remember the long way that the Lord your God has led you these forty years in the wilderness, in order to humble you, testing you to know what was in your heart, whether or not you would keep his commandments.

Psalm 105:5 (NRSV)

Remember the wonderful works he has done, his miracles, and the judgments he has uttered...

Message of Hope:

One day, I stumbled upon a video that told a story about the value of remembering the journey to destiny. As the video began, a very successful husband and wife were strolling along the street and the wife recognized an old high school friend who had become a construction worker. The wife and friend were happy to see each other and she introduced him to her husband. The conversation ended and as the couple walked away, the husband said "aren't you glad you married me and not that guy? You wouldn't have half of the things you have now if you had hooked up with him!"

The wife reminded her husband of their lifestyle before he became successful. They lived in a small apartment, but they were in love and happy. The wife supported her husband while he was in college. She reminded him of how he didn't know how to dress for interviews or make a nice tie and she helped him. They struggled to make ends meet each day as he slowly rose to the top of his profession. Shaken by this trip down memory lane, the husband apologized for his inconsiderate comments about his wife's friend.

Does this story bring back memories for you? Would you judge a person by their situation without recognizing your cynical ways? Have you become so accustomed to your blessings that you've forgotten life hasn't always been so good? You may not be a millionaire today, but you are probably a long ways from where you were a few years ago. Every struggle leads us to our destiny. When we reach the life we have dreamed of, we must never forget where we've come from when we encounter someone who is still walking in their challenges.

Every test and every hard time is an important piece of your journey. As mentioned in Deuteronomy 8:2, trials are allowed in our lives to reveal the depth of our love and trust in God. He wants to know if you will trust Him in season (when life feels good) and out of season (when trials come). When you come through all of those hard trials, remember them as stepping stones to the destiny God has designed for you.

Prayer:

Father, I don't ever want to forget Your goodness and mercy towards me! You are an awesome God! Every trial and struggle I have come through is a testimony of Your presence in my life! God, I pray I never forget how far I've come by the Grace of God! I trust and pray by the power of Jesus, Your Son, and in His Name! Amen!

Think About It:

If it had not been for the Lord on my side...where would I be?
Through every trial and every challenge God has been there for me.
May I never forget all that He's done for me!
Thank You, God, for the journey to my destiny!

Listen...

No Hocus Pocus

Scripture:

Luke 6:38 (NRSV)

...give, and it will be given to you. A good measure, pressed down, shaken together, running over, will be put into your lap; for the measure you give will be the measure you get back.

Message of Hope:

A friend once told me about the good things God had provided. God blessed them so well that they were able to help a family member with a large sum of money. Once they obeyed God by extravagant giving, God returned the favor with a mighty blessing.

When I shared my friend's story with someone, I was told the story sounded like an example of "voodoo religion." There are some people who believe others only give to see what God will give them in return. You know, if you say all the "right words" or act in the "right way," you will get a bountiful blessing. Sincerity doesn't have to play an important part in this kind of giving. Just "act" right, even if it's fake, and you will get a blessing!

Our faith can become "voodoo" or "hocus-pocus" faith if we do the right things only to get what we can from God. Our God is not a "voodoo" or "hocus pocus" God. We cannot trick God into blessing us.

If we seek first the kingdom of God (His will and desire for us), He will add blessings in our lives. The Word of God commands us to bless others without expecting anything in return. God sees us when we bless others and will, in turn, bless us for our acts of sincere generosity. So, blessings are not fake or magical. Blessings are a real demonstration of God's love.

When we go to God in our private time of prayer and make our needs and desires known to Him, He will bless us openly. Other people may get the whole blessing thing twisted by thinking whatever gain you have received, you got it by your own abilities or you were just lucky. There's no luck or happenstance involved. When God is ready to bless you, He will bless you in His own intentional way!

Prayer:

Thank You God for the many blessings you bestow! Every breath I take and everything I have the grace and strength to achieve comes directly from You! I pray that I always regard what I have with reverence and honor to the Giver of All Things! It is in the Strong Name of Jesus, I trust, believe, and pray! Amen!!

Think About It:

Be faithful in all things simply for the sake of being faithful!
The blessings will come when we give with a grateful and cheerful heart!
God is in the blessing business!

Listen...

The Joys of Giving

Scripture:

Philippians 4:19 (NRSV)

And my God will fully satisfy every need of yours according to his riches in glory in Christ Jesus.

Mark 4:24 (NRSV)

And he said to them, "Pay attention to what you hear; the measure you give will be the measure you get, and still more will be given..."

Message of Hope:

Giving is one of my most favorite things to do! I love to give gifts! So, birthdays, Christmas, Boss' Day, and sometimes for no special reason, I find joy in choosing the right gift for someone special! For me, it is so rewarding to know my gift added happiness to another person's day! To be able to bless a friend, family member, or even a stranger with something they need makes the giving worthwhile!

The giving of my time, talent, treasure, and help to my church is another great joy! Why? Well, let me tell you...I haven't always been equipped to give financially. Many times, the best I could give seemed so very small. There were times I wanted to be active in giving and couldn't because I was serving my family as a caregiver. I've had holidays when I could not give to my church, family, or friends because finances were low.

God has blessed me through it all and I am compelled by His generosity to give as much as possible! When called upon to serve God's people, I get excited about the opportunity! Now, when birthdays and holidays roll around, it gives me joy to give careful and considerate gifts! Sometimes, the Holy Spirit will prompt me to give a gift...just because!

Beloved, the act of giving and the ability to give is a blessing modeled after the ultimate gift of Jesus! We cannot out-give God! The Word reminds us that God willingly gave us His Son because He loved us so much! There's no better gift than the redemptive gift of the sacrifice of Jesus!

Oh, and don't worry about your own stockpile of stuff! Don't let the thought of lack block you from being a giver. God smiles on those who give with a sincere heart. Have you ever watched how your popcorn is stuffed in the bag at the movies? Just when you think it's full, they shake the bag and press it down to make room for more...until the popcorn is running over! That's just how God works! Every time you give, He will pour more grace, goodness, love, and mercy into your life until you are running over with the blessings of God!

God's word promises He will satisfy your needs. If you truly NEED it, He's got it!

Prayer:

God, Thank You for never getting tired of giving to me my daily needs and even the desires of my heart that aligns with Your will! The gift of Your Son Jesus is something I will never forget! Thank You for an abundance of Your Grace and Love! It is in the Strong Name of Jesus, I trust, believe, and pray! Amen!

Think About It:

Exercise those giving muscles and watch the goodness of God explode in your life! Give yourself away (wisely) and let Him use you for His glory!

Listen...

The Prayers that Carry Us Through

Scripture:

Ephesians 6:18 (NRSV)

Pray in the Spirit at all times in every prayer and supplication.
To that end keep alert and always persevere in supplication for all the saints.

James 5:16 (NRSV)

Therefore confess your sins to one another, and pray for one another, so that you may be healed. The prayer of the righteous is powerful and effective.

Message of Hope:

Have you ever taken a moment to think of the blessings that come from the prayers of others? Every time you come through a challenge victoriously, it is partly due to someone praying for you. My mother would constantly remind me that she would mention me in prayer at least three times a day! It was such a comfort to my soul to know I was covered in prayer!

When we pray for others, we are simply obeying God's word. Because God has clothed us in righteousness, the prayers of the righteous are effective! God will honor your prayers for others by also blessing you in unexpected measure. Intercessory prayer, pleading someone else's case to God, displays our genuine love and concern for others.

We would probably be amazed at the number of people who sincerely and diligently pray for us without ceasing! Try praying for someone else and you will discover all of the blessings you have enjoyed through the prayers of others!

Prayer:

Father, Thank You for putting me on someone else's mind and heart that they would pray for me! God, I know for sure that someone somewhere has prayed for me when I couldn't pray for myself! I am also so grateful to Your Son, Jesus, who sits at Your Right Side interceding for us! With gratitude and in Your Son's Name, I pray! Amen!

Think About It:

Thank You God for every prayer warrior who has lifted my cause to You! Teach me to be selfless in prayer.
May my prayers help someone make it through their challenges to attain their God ordained destiny!

Listen...

The Promise

Scripture:

Isaiah 40:31 (NRSV)

...but those who wait for the Lord shall renew their strength, they shall mount up with wings like eagles, they shall run and not be weary, they shall walk and not faint.

Isaiah 41:10 (NRSV)

...do not fear, for I am with you,
do not be afraid, for I am your God;
I will strengthen you, I will help you,
I will uphold you with my victorious right hand.

Message of Hope:

Sometimes, events in life can throw you off course and cause you to forget the promises of God. While it may be well intended, family and friends can make promises that may be broken. Surely, we cannot rely on the promises of others who are susceptible to failure.

The Word of God is replete of His divine promises and those promises are everlasting! When we trust in His word and rely on God, we will find He is our true Father, Protector, Provider and Friend. His word promises us strength and energy for every task and challenge. He promises to be our Helper in the time of need and our Battle Axe against every foe. Even as the Son of God was preparing for His trial and death, He left the promise: "And I will ask the Father, and he will give you another advocate to be with you forever." (John 14:16) Jesus knew we would need comfort and guidance and left the promise of the Holy Spirit to be with us.

If you need healing for your body, mind or soul, God has promised to be your Healer! If you need a blessing of any kind, seek God first and He will add good things to your life. Our God promises to give us peace in troubling times and wisdom in every test. God promises to supply everything we need. Seek God's plan for you through His Word and in prayer. He really does have the solution and a promise to every problem we face! When you seek Him with all your heart, you will discover God has never made a promise He did not keep.

Prayer:

Father, I trust and depend on Your promises. While I may have strayed from You from time to time, You have never left me. I thank You for Your promise to be my Mother, Father, Friend and Comforter. There is no covering better, stronger, or more vast than the covering of Your wings of divine love! Thank You God for Your undying promises. It is in the strong and loving Name of Jesus, I pray! Amen!

Think About It:

I'm standing on the promises of God
Through faith and hope, His promises will prevail!
My trust is in the Great Promise Keeper!

Listen...

Walking in the Shadow

Scripture:

Psalm 36:7 (NRSV)

How precious is your steadfast love, O God! All people may take refuge in the shadow of your wings.

Message of Hope:

There have been many times in life I have asked God to walk with me. As years go on, I have begun to think it would be awesome to simply walk in His shadow. There is mercy and grace in His shadow because He is covering our path before we even take one step! His shadow provides a shield of protection.

The Word of God warns us that the true presence of God would be too overwhelming for us to handle. Walking in His shadow provides the assurance that where we are headed will be a safe place where peace and joy abides. In His shadow, all of the fiery darts of the enemy are absorbed by the Lord! The path of God's shadow is a prepared place where God has cleared the way for us to proceed without worry or anxiety!

Life can be difficult and full of many challenges, choices and mind boggling decisions! Walking in God's shadow demonstrates our willingness to let God control every situation.

Prayer:

Father, I am grateful to walk in Your shadow! In the shade of Your protection, there is peace and Your glory! I don't need a spotlight! I simply need to be covered by Your wings! It is in the Mighty Name of Jesus, I pray and Thank You! Amen!

Think About It:

Lead me, Jesus, in the shadow of Your love.
Let Your glory guide my steps.
Hide me, protect, prepare me in Your shadow!

Listen...

You Are a Piece of Work

Scripture:

Psalm 139:14 (NRSV)

I praise you, for I am fearfully and wonderfully made.
Wonderful are your works, that I know very well.

Psalm 100:3 (NRSV)

Know that the Lord is God.
It is He that made us, and we are his;
we are His people, and the sheep of his pasture.

Message of Hope:

You've probably heard the phrase "He or she is a piece of work!" This is not meant as a flattering remark. It is usually spoken out of frustration from someone's actions. When someone is a "piece of work," they are being difficult, acting odd, or just not responding at our level of expectation.

In contrast, when we consider the creativity of God, every person is a piece of work carved out by the great Creator. I know it may be a challenge, but try to imagine the most difficult person as a piece of God's handiwork. Now, God didn't create them to act out or be disruptive. Those characteristics are not from God. But, every good characteristic is there...it just may be hiding because a destructive spirit has taken rule.

Every person was created by God for a divine purpose. It is up to us to be available and willing to hear from God and identify our purpose. Just as a fine work of art or a beautiful pearl; our gifts and talents are heavenly treasures placed in us to bless the earth and glorify God!

The next time someone irritates you, look for the hidden good in them. If it is not easy to see, remember everyone was created by God. He gives us free will to live and act as we choose. No one is perfect, but all of us are dear to God's heart as one of His greatest creations!

Prayer:

God, Thank You for creating me! Thank You for all of the gifts and talents You placed in me that I may not even see! Father, I pray for the ability to offer grace as I view others! Help me to point them to the person You created that they may give You Glory! In the Matchless Name of Jesus, I pray! Amen!

Think About It:

Beneath the layers of the me that I present to others each day lies the masterful work of my Heavenly Father!
He does all things well!

Listen...

Don't Throw In the Towel

Scripture:

1 Corinthians 10:13 (NRSV)

No testing has overtaken you that is not common to everyone.
God is faithful, and he will not let you be tested beyond your strength,
but with the testing he will also provide the way out so that you may
be able to endure it.

Message of Hope:

It can be devastating to hear someone seriously declare they want to end
it all. Hard times will fall upon all of us at some point in our lifetime.
Disappointments and failures could leave you in distress and with a
sense of worthlessness. As difficult as things may become, do not test
fate. Our present and futures are in the hands of God. Even in times
of great despair, God can help you get through it to arrive at the side
of victory!

If we maintain our focus on God and become determined to recognize
His love for us, we will see that we are wonderful and complex creations
of God. He can look beyond our faults and love us regardless of our
sin. If we learn to rest in our awareness of God's power, He will renew
our strength!

Life is a gift that also comes with tests. There is no challenge you will
face that has not presented its pain to someone else. In our humanity,
we can so easily succumb to temptations that lead us down the wrong

path. There is power in the promise of God's Word to keep us through the struggle.

Mistakes and disappointments have a way of leaving scars on our hearts and minds, convincing us that we are insignificant or losers. Once those kind of thoughts set up camp in our psyche, we could become detached from all that we know to be righteous and true about our Heavenly Father and ourselves.

Regardless the of loss, betrayal, mistakes or misjudgments, God still loves you and will not allow these things to utterly destroy you. Your life has a purpose and God has a plan! He will protect His plan for you. You cannot give up now! You could be just one day or one minute away from your breakthrough! There's a future waiting for you! Don't throw in the towel!

Prayer:

Father, when it seems like everything is falling apart, I stretch my hands to You! Help me in my weakest times to keep the faith and trust in You! In the Powerful Name of Jesus, I lean, trust, and pray! Amen!

Think About It:

It's not over until God says it's over!
Keep fighting! Keep praying! Keep trusting in your God!
He will always provide a way out!

Listen...

Control

Scripture:

Genesis 12:1-4

1 Now the Lord said to Abram, "Go from your country and your kindred and your father's house to the land that I will show you.
2 I will make of you a great nation, and I will bless you, and make your name great, so that you will be a blessing.
3 I will bless those who bless you, and the one who curses you I will curse; and in you all the families of the earth shall be blessed."
4 So Abram, went, as the Lord had told him; and Lot went with him. Abram was seventy-five years old when he departed from Haran.

Message of Hope:

Have you ever used the phrase "I'm in control." Perhaps you have, at some point, asked the question "Who's in control?" The reality is that God has the ultimate control over every element of our lives and the world. In our human frailties, we may fall into the delusion of believing we are the ones in full control. In fact, most of us avoid certain opportunities or responsibilities because we will not have the level of control we desire.

Recognizing God as the One in control is a major step along the journey of faith. God may bless us with homes, families, talents, and multiple streams of income but we are simply stewards over these things. God trusts us to take care of our gifts, but we are not in control of them.

At the age of 75, Abram's life was turned upside down when God instructed him to leave his father's home. He had no idea where he would be going or end up. Abram had to allow God to have full control. There were many other times when Abram's only choice was to yield to God's request. Now, Abram made some mistakes along his life's journey but he would always come back to his belief that God was in full control and God knew the plan for his life.

The Bible has many stories of prophets and others who yielded control to God and He blessed them with guidance and abundance. Esther thought the only element of her destiny was to be queen until Mordecai convinced her to stand up for her people. Once she stepped into her true destiny, God took control and changed the fate of Esther, Mordecai and their people. Ruth gained a husband and a position in the lineage of Jesus when she allowed God to have control of her life's trajectory. Abraham (Abram) became the father of many nations when he allowed God to have control of his life. Moses faltered in his leadership at times, but he learned how to let God have control. Jesus was willing to serve others, accept ridicule and suffer death on the cross because He knew His Heavenly Father had everything under control.

When life seems out of control, give the situation to God in prayer. Don't worry. Trust God's ways. He knows far more than we do! His way of solving our problems will bring out His best that resides in us!

Prayer:

God, I yield all control to You! As the Creator of my life and this world, You know what's best for me! When my faith grows weak, I will cry out to You for help! Increase Yourself in me oh God so that I will follow You! In the Incredible Name of Jesus, I pray! Amen!

Think About It:

There are things about tomorrow we may not understand.
Let God be in control of tomorrow.
Let God take the lead and hold your hand.

Listen...

Granny's Song

Scripture:

Matthew 11:28-29 (NRSV)

28 Come to me, all you that are weary and are carrying heavy burdens, and I will give you rest.
29 Take my yoke upon you, and learn from me; for I am gentle and humble in heart, and you will find rest for your souls.

Message of Hope:

This message is dedicated to the memory of my dear Grandmother, Elsie Mae Ruff. Granny (as I called her) loved the hymn "Come Ye Disconsolate." After several years and a few challenges in life, I began to understand why this was Granny's favorite hymn.

As I heard a great preacher quote the lyrics at the end of a sermon, I realized every word of the hymn affirms that there is nothing too hard for God. I'm sure Granny had many challenges and sorrows that I never knew. Granny made it through every test of life with the assurance that earth had no sorrow or calamity that Heaven could not help her overcome! I am certain she found rest for her weary mind, body and soul when she relied on God.

This great hymn of the church reminds us that our troubles are no challenge for God! How much simpler life would be if we remembered the power of God as our champion over the trying storms of life. Whatever our problems; God can solve them! There's healing, rest and comfort available at the Mercy Seat of God and you can find Him through prayer, worship, and the word of God!

Thank you Granny for being a strong example of strength and grace. Now I know you were able to stand through all of life's storms with the assurance God would walk with you.

Prayer:

Thank You God for Your Mercy Seat, the place of prayer and healing! I am so grateful that we can bring all of our distress, grief, struggles and wounds to You! Truly You are an Awesome God! It is in the Name of Jesus, I pray and give You praise! Amen!

Think About It:

Come ye disconsolate
Where ever ye languish
Come to the mercy seat
Fervently kneel
Here bring your wounded hearts
Here tell your anguish
Earth has no sorrow that Heaven cannot heal

(*Come Ye Disconsolate*, Thomas Moore, The Methodist Hymnal, Hymn 103, 1966)

Listen...

How Deep is Your Love?

Scripture:

1 Corinthians 13:4-7 (NRSV)

4 Love is patient; love is kind; love is not envious or boastful or arrogant
5 or rude. It does not insist on its own way; it is not irritable or resentful;
6 It does not rejoice in wrongdoing, but rejoices in truth.
7 It bears all things, believes all things, hopes all things, endures all things.

Message of Hope:

"I love you!" These three words are quite often spoken without consideration of the huge impact they can have on someone's life. Authentic love extends beyond feelings. Love is attached to responsibility and loyalty and even surpasses circumstances!

The biblical definition of love can help us remain true to our commitment of love toward others. God loves us so much and makes Himself available to supply every need we have according to His glorious riches. God's love is patient and forgiving. He allowed His only Son, Jesus, to die for us while we were still wallowing in our sins. If God can love us to such a great degree, surely we can try to love others following His example.

How deep is your love? Do you exercise patience and kindness towards others? Can you endure with others even when they get on your nerves? Hopefully, you do not place yourself above anyone because of the advantages and depth of your blessings. Prayerfully, you are not envious of someone else's blessings. When we fully extend ourselves to love, we will not get excited when a brother or sister falls. We believe in everything that is true; we believe for the best against all odds; and hang in there with hope for those we love.

Does your love for someone match these characteristics spelled out in the word of God? The greatest expression of thanksgiving is shown through our love for God and those He has placed in our lives. Showing your love is not limited to showering people with tangible gifts. Sometimes, the best gift of love is a prayer, a thoughtful act, words of appreciation or just being present. The next time you tell someone "I love you," consider the depth of your words and the sincerity of your actions.

Prayer:

Father, the depth of my love for You can never compare to Your love for me. Help me to love others sincerely and fully as I am led by Your example and Your word. It is in the Loving Name of Jesus, I pray! Amen!

Think About It:

What would my life look like without the Love of God?!

Listen...

Is There Any Hope?

Scripture:

Jeremiah 29:11 (NRSV)

For surely I know the plans I have for you, says the Lord, plans for your welfare and not harm, to give you a future with hope

Romans 5:5 (NSRV)

...and hope does not disappoint us, because God's love has been poured into our hearts through the Holy Spirit that has been given to us.

Message of Hope:

Have you ever had an experience that left you feeling hopeless? If not yet, the day will come when you may discover your hope factor is at a deficit. Now, I know Christians are taught to never give up hope. Sometimes, challenges can be so rough that you forget to play your "I'm a Hope-Filled Christian" card! Well, perhaps by the time these messages are published, most people who pick up this book will have lived through the COVID-19 pandemic. That is a true testament of living by faith and hope!

Hope is something we must fight for with every ounce of our being. We must strive daily to keep the hope of Christ alive. Christ's love and God's desire to bless us will never fade away. Jeremiah was chosen by God to be a prophet at a young age. He was doubtful that he was suitable for the task. God knew differently because He knew the plans

He had in store. The promise of hope given to Jeremiah remains for us today.

When your hope begins to fade, just think about the things God has already done. Consider His track record! You have made it through every valley experience by His grace! In disappointment and failure, God was right there...even when you couldn't feel His presence! Keep your Hope alive in prayer, worship, and the Word of God!

If times ever seem dark and empty, I promise you...God is right there beside you! God has assigned the Holy Spirit to guide and sustain you! Keep your Hope alive!

Prayer:

Father, Thank You for hope and a future! Thank You for Your love that flows to us by the power of the Holy Spirit! I press forward in Your Truth and Your Hope for me! In the Powerful Name of Jesus, I pray! Amen!

Think About It:

Whatever the situation, I stand in my belief that God is near!
Hope is my helper and Hope is my sustainer!
My Hope is in God!

Listen...

It's Just Like Christmas Eve!

Scripture:

Psalm 23 (NRSV)

The Lord is my shepherd, I shall not want.
He makes me lie down in green pastures;
    he leads me beside still waters; he restores my soul. He leads me in
    right paths for his name's sake.
Even though I walk through the darkest valley, I fear no evil; for you
are with me;
    your rod and your staff—they comfort me.
You prepare a table before me in the presence of my enemies;
    you anoint my head with oil; my cup overflows.
Surely goodness and mercy shall follow me all the days of my life,
    and I shall dwell in the house of the Lord my whole life long.

Message of Hope:

One mid-September evening not so long ago, I heard God speak to my
spirit "it's just like Christmas Eve!" Huh? It's September! Nevertheless, I
was compelled to listen for what He had to say! Then He led me to Psalm
23. Some of us can pray this Psalm without thinking about it because
it has been infused into our spirit and memory. I can imagine someone
right now saying "what does Psalm 23 have to do with Christmas Eve?"

Christmas Eve was an exciting time in my childhood days! My parents
LOVED Christmas and the house was busy with preparation! Food was
being prepped. My Dad was making his famous egg nog and my Mom
was making her best sweet potatoes and mac-n-cheese. In between

cooking, we were wrapping gifts, leaving my gifts for later. The good china was pulled out and the silverware was polished. Every room in the house was cleaned up and ready for family to arrive. I was so excited, I barely slept that night! The next day, gifts were waiting to be opened and I would be overjoyed by the splendor of the day!

So, just before God spoke Christmas Eve to my spirit, He said "2021!" You know, perhaps "It's just like Christmas Eve" was actually my response to His statement. God was saying "I'm preparing you and everyone for 2021...every day leading up to it and even every day after 2021!"

It would be nice to know exactly what the future will bring, but I don't have a crystal ball and God hasn't shown me all of the details, but He did tell me He's preparing us...right now! Every day that you wake up is a day of preparation! So, just like my parents did all the work ALL night long Christmas Eve preparing for Christmas Day...God has been and is still working to prepare us for new and brighter days!

When life seems to get uglier almost every day, God is working. If someone's hurtful actions breaks your heart, God is behind the scenes clearing up some things. Financial woes, relationship struggles, stress and out-of-control situations are no challenge for God. Just take some deep breaths and allow Him to restore your soul for the next task. Rest and allow God to lead you to the right path. He will anoint you with His oil and make your cup overflow.

Strange, difficult, and hurtful times are a part of life. Through it all, God is preparing great things for us. In the season of preparation, His goodness and His mercy will follow us. Great things will happen, even in the valley of despair. God will dwell in us and we can dwell with Him!

Prayer:

God, I Thank You for preparing me! When life seems too much to bear, I will look to You. I know You will provide rest, protection from my enemies, and peace to my soul. Thank You God for being a Father, Provider and Deliverer! In the Mighty Name of Jesus, I trust and pray. Amen!

Think About It:

He's preparing me for something I cannot handle right now
He's making me ready
Just because He cares
He's providing me with what I'll need to carry out the next matter in my life
Preparing me For everything that comes in my life
He is preparing you
God is preparing us
He's providing me with what I'll need
Because He cares for me, God is preparing me!

(*He's Preparing Me* by Daryl Coley)

Listen...

Just Visiting

Scripture:

2 Corinthians 5:9-10 (NRSV)

9 So whether we are at home or away, we make it our aim to please him. 10 For all of us must appear before the judgment seat of Christ, so that each may receive recompense for what has been done in the body, whether good or evil.

Message of Hope

Wherever I travel, I like to survey the land and get a sense of the vibe of the area I am visiting. I want to know everything about the area. Is it safe to walk the streets alone? Where are the good restaurants and prime shopping opportunities? On one visit, I needed to know the location of the nearest hospital. I want to know all of the resources I may need during my visit in a new location and learn as much as possible about my surroundings.

We could consider our time on earth as a visit also. How we use our time here is important to glorify God and build a legacy established and developed by faith. You see, God expects us to be fruitful and multiply while we are here to make the most of our visit, wherever life may take us. God wants us to use the life we have been given by blessing others and being examples of His mercy and grace.

Some of us may leave earthly treasures behind for family and friends. Our heirs may cherish these items or soon discard them. After all, material things don't last a lifetime. The impact we have had on the life of another will extend beyond the importance of earthly treasures.

As visitors on earth, let us daily consider our mission to be a blessing to someone else. Life means so much more than gathering up treasures that will eventually fade away. Our service to God through showing love and patience to others will also draw us closer to God and our divine purpose. A giving and loving heart makes the visit worthwhile for the host and the guest!

Prayer:

God, while on this earthly journey, it is my desire to please You! I pray that my life shows others the possibilities of the Grace and Mercy of God! None of us knows how long we will live, but I hope I live a life that shines with the light of Jesus! In the Life Giving Name of Jesus, I pray! Amen!

Think About It:

May the way I live show the presence of God!
May the service I give show the compassion of God's heart!
When I stand before my God, I want to hear Him say "Well done!"
Then my time on earth will not have been in vain!

Listen...

Living a Free Life

Scripture:

John 8:36 (NRSV)

So if the Son makes you free, you will be free indeed.

Message of Hope:

Some people achieve their sense of importance by dominating others. When folks can keep you in your place, they feel superior and secure. Their definition of you keeps you within the boundaries they have created for you. Beloved, it's time to free yourself from the opinions and control of others!

Some of us create our own limitations based on the opinions of others. What are your self-perceived limits or boundaries? Self-doubt, the fear of failure and the anticipation of ridicule or judgment can stifle the possibilities of your destiny. You know what God has called you to do but you keep denying it because you've been told you're not smart enough, good-looking enough, rich enough or you just don't have what it takes! What if you make a mistake? What if no one listens to you? Whether the personal limitations hanging over your life are ones you conjured up or others determined for you, it's time to be free!

It's time to grab ahold of the freedom given to you by Christ! He came to this earth and withstood disrespect, suffering and undeserved humiliation to give us freedom from guilt and shame! Don't waste this freedom! Reject the limits, boxes, and destiny blockers you or others impose on your future! Through Christ, you are free from doubt, shame and fear! You are free to soar!

Prayer:

God, Thank You for sending Your Son to give me freedom in the here and now! There is no power on earth than can block the blessings you have ordained for my life! In the Freeing Name of Jesus, I live, trust, serve, and pray! Amen!

Think About It:

Praise the Lord! I am free!
The power of the redemptive resurrection of Christ frees me to be the Child of God I am destined to be!

Listen...

Good Company

Scripture:

Matthew 18:20 (NRSV)

For where two or three are gathered in my name, I am there among them.

1 Peter 4:10 (NRSV)

Like good stewards of the manifold grace of God, serve one another with whatever gift each of you has received.

Message of Hope:

This message pays tribute to my dear cousin Van Hughes. Van passed away many years ago, but I will always remember him as the good company I needed as an only child of older parents. I was not allowed to wander off the front porch. My friends could visit me, but I could not visit them as often as I would like. So, I had a lot of alone time on that porch.

My cousin Van was older than me, but he didn't like seeing his little cousin alone. He would occasionally walk to my house with chips and soda for each of us and we would sit on my front steps. We never had a lot of conversation because Van was a very quiet and gentle soul. We simply enjoyed each other's company.

Good company shares your likes and dislikes and will allow you to simply relax and be yourself. When we seek to be comforting, encouraging and supportive, we are serving the other person with the gifts we have received from God. As noted in 1 Peter 4:10, we become good stewards of God's grace when we share our gifts.

Begin each day with the desire to be good company for someone who is alone, struggling with a challenge, or simply hopes a visit or call will brighten the day. Celebrate a friend or loved one's achievement! Stand close to a friend during a tough time. Get excited about being the good company that eases a soul in distress.

Allow God to direct you to a good company crew that connects to hold each other up when times are rough and celebrate when days are brighter! Whether the crew is two or three showing God's love to each other, He will be in the middle of the group.

Prayer:

Father, Thank You for those You have placed in my life to be my good company. I am grateful for their encouragement and love. It is my prayer that I will pursue good stewardship by sharing your love with others. It is in the Precious Name of Jesus, I pray! Amen!

Think About It:

Being good company gives us the opportunity to show others the love of God!

Listen...

How Hungry Are You?

Scripture:

Matthew 5:6 (NRSV)

Blessed are those who hunger and thirst for righteousness, for they will be filled.

Message of Hope:

Have you ever been hungry for something in particular? Once you enjoyed it, it was probably everything you had been hungry for and more! Well, may I ask you to consider your hunger for all God desires for you and all He wants you to do for others.

Along life's journey to destiny, I wonder how much we really want to get to our destiny. Are we so desperately hungry to be a blessing that we will do the work necessary to get there or would we rather half-step our way and be satisfied with just a few blessings in our lifetime.

To satisfy the unique hunger for the right things of God, we must spend some time with Him, listen for His voice and follow His instructions. We can develop a hunger for righteousness when we seek to be a blessing to those who are hungry for care, encouragement, joy, renewed hope, and help through trying times. Seeking righteousness will not go unnoticed by God. The word of God promises blessings and satisfaction to those who desire to do the right things of God. Lives can be changed for the better and we will grow in faith as we fulfill our hunger to do God's will!

Prayer:

Father, I hunger and thirst for Your righteousness! Strengthen and equip me to do Your will. I pray to become the hope, light, and help for a weary, hungry soul. It is in the Powerful Name of Jesus, I pray! Amen!

Think About It:

We can make this world a better place!
We can help others champion life's challenges!
We can become beacons of God's righteousness!

Listen...

There Is a Sisterhood of Strength

Scripture:

Romans 15:1-2 (NRSV)

1 We who are strong ought to put up with the failings of the weak, and not to please ourselves.
2 Each of us must please His neighbor for the good purpose of building up the neighbor.

Message of Hope:

Women possess a peculiar strength that enables them to simultaneously endure many things; achieve goals; and fulfill obligations. Actually, this is a God-ordained strength available to everyone. David called upon this gift of strength in Psalm 18:2 "The Lord is my rock, and my fortress, and my deliverer; my God, my rock in whom I take refuge, my shield...."

Back to the sisters! Many of us work in and outside of the home, caring for family and friends and holding down job duties while maintaining a special grace and beauty only made possible by the Creator. We have the ability to bear and nurture children, literally introducing life to the world and grooming others to become productive contributors to society.

There is even greater strength to be found when women identify each other as sisters. Sharing in each other's pain, joys, sadness, and doubts creates a sisterhood of strength and grace. This bond can alleviate the anguish of feeling alone in our struggles or uncelebrated in times of joy.

Supporting each other for the good of each other makes the sisterhood real and helps all of us to thrive!

Prayer:

Father, Thank You for giving us each other to love and support! I pray we show our love for You in the way we love others! In Jesus' Mighty Name, we pray! Amen!

Think About It:

Lord, help us to be our Sister's and our Brother's keeper!
Teach us to bear each other's burdens, share in each other's joy and grow in faith through unity!

Listen...

The Blessing in Front of You

Scripture:

Amos 5:4-6a (NRSV)

4 For thus says the Lord to the house of Israel: Seek me and live;
5 but do not seek Bethel, and do not enter into Gilgal or cross over to
Beer-Sheba; for Gilgal shall surely go into exile, and Bethel shall come
to nothing.
6 Seek the Lord and live...

Message of Hope:

If you have never put something down and forgot where you put it, don't
worry, sooner or later it will happen! One day I put my glasses down and
became so busy in a task that I forgot where I placed the glasses when I
tried to find them. I thought I had thrown the glasses in the trash! Two
weeks had gone by and I decided to schedule an early eye exam to get
new glasses. I gave up on what was assumed to be lost.

One night I went to a table to pick up my phone, looked up at a nearby
floor lamp and my glasses were hanging on the side of the lamp! You can
imagine how happy I was to discover those glasses! Now, my husband
was standing by waiting for me to see the glasses. He answered, "they
were hanging on the lamp all along!"

Of course, once he told me, I remembered placing the glasses on the
lamp "for a quick moment!" Ok, I can envision the big laugh you just
had from reading this story! It's ok, enjoy your laugh!

When your vision is misguided or cloudy, you could miss the blessings that have been right in front of you all along. When you are distracted, blessings could be right under your nose! Looking at the scripture, Bethel, Gilgal and Beer-Sheba were places where people worshipped idols and looked to material things instead of looking to God!

Quite often, we look for peace, joy, and love in all the wrong places, people, and things. All of the things your soul desires are right in front of you, or should I say they are right inside of you. Your Heavenly Father, and all of the blessings He can offer, are closer than each breath you take.

Don't wander around looking in the wrong places for the right thing. Only a relationship with God can offer the priceless gift of His love, protection, provision and life! Beloved, He has been right in front of you and will never leave your side.

Prayer:

Father, Thank You for Your guidance when I am lost. Thank You for Your protection and provision when I am in need. Thank You for life, hope, and peace when it seems like everything around me is falling apart. There is no other way to live than with Your love. In Jesus' Name, I trust and pray! Amen!

Think About It:

When I am sad
When I am lost
When I am searching for the joys of the Spirit
The blessings of God are closer than the air I breathe

Listen...

The Fight Against Evil

Scripture:

Ephesians 6:10-18 (NRSV)

10 Finally, be strong in the Lord and in the strength of his power.

11 Put on the whole armor of God, so that you may be able to stand against the wiles of the devil.

12 For our struggle is not against enemies of blood and flesh, but against the rulers, against the authorities, against the cosmic powers of this present darkness, against the spiritual forces of evil in the heavenly places.

13 Therefore take up the whole armor of God, so that you may be able to withstand on that evil day, and having done everything, to stand firm.

14 Stand therefore, and fasten the belt of truth around your waist, and put on the breastplate of righteousness.

15 As shoes for your feet put on whatever will make you ready to proclaim the gospel of peace.

16 With all of these, take the shield of faith, with which you will be able to quench all the flaming arrows of the evil one.

17 Take the helmet of salvation, and the sword of the Spirit, which is the word of God.

18 Pray in the Spirit at all times in every prayer and supplication. To that end keep alert and always persevere in supplication for all the saints.

Message of Hope:

This message is not for the faint of heart! If life seems to be all together wonderful for you at this moment, don't be fooled into thinking all is right and wonderful with the world. Evil is always lurking about seeking to wreak havoc and discord. All things evil have been at war with righteousness since the beginning of time. While evil has lost many fights, to include death, the battle continues. The rulers of evil understand that their time is winding up. There will be a day when righteousness will reign supreme.

The primary weapon of evil is the control of your mind. If the ruler of every evil thing can take up space in our minds, the fight continues between good and evil. Tricks of the enemy's trade such as the actions and words of other people will cause you to doubt your relationship with God. It may also cause you to question the Word of God. Attitudes and personalities will rise up to inflict chaos and despair.

The struggle is real but God reminds us in His word that we are equipped for this battle against evil. We have the power to fight the demons of this world. Trust God! Be determined to keep your focus on Him! If you slip away, run back to God in prayer. You can totally ask Him to help you and He will keep you from falling!

If you have not proclaimed Jesus as your Savior, do it now and your mind will be protected by His salvation. Be dressed in your faith daily and cover yourself, your family and all loved ones in prayer. Protect your life with the righteousness of God. Ask Him to guide your feet in every step you make. Remember, the person attacking you is not the demon. They are just under demonic control. This may seem spooky and scary, but it is a reality of this world. The Word of God warns us of evil residing in high places. Ask God for guidance and discernment to enable you to identify evil and fight it by the power of prayer and the work of the Holy Spirit!

Prayer:

Father, I ask you to help me when evil tries to knock me down and distract me! I pray that I remember to call upon Your Word, Wisdom, Mercy and Grace! I am not perfect, but I do serve and trust a perfect God! In the Forgiving Name of Jesus, I pray! Amen!

Think About It:

Evil does not have the final say!
I live and breathe in the faith and power of The Almighty!
My God will prevail and deliver us from ALL evil!

Listen...

There's a Blessing in the Burden

Scripture:

Psalm 55:22 (NRSV)

Cast your burden on the Lord, and he will sustain you;
He will never permit the righteous to be moved.

Message of Hope:

Although it may be difficult to accept, there is a blessing in every burden. When challenges come our way, we may not be able to easily imagine the other side of the burden. We can become so deeply focused on the hardship the burden presents that we miss the message in the process. Trying times can leave us feeling drained and hopeless while God is in the middle of it all with grace and strength for us to endure.

Every burden that comes our way is accompanied with a specific lesson. Burdens help to build character while testing our faith. The season of burdens will show you how much you depend on God and how much more your faith must be stretched.

Becoming a caregiver, single parenting, enduring a health or financial challenge, or having your intellect challenged are burdens I'm sure none of us want to experience. All kinds of challenges will pop up in life. God will teach you how to champion all of them if you remain open to the will of God for you. Burdens will bring out characteristics in you like you never imagined!

There is a blessing deep within every burden. God will not leave us to deal with the burdens alone. I promise you, as I also remind myself, you will come out on the other side of the burden stronger, wiser, and better!

Prayer:

Father, I depend on Your Grace and Mercy when burdens try to get the best of me. I pray for Your strength to endure it all knowing there are blessings deep within my burdens. In the Comforting Name of Jesus, I pray! Amen!

Think About It:

When I feel weak beneath the pressures of heavy burdens,
Father let the hand of Jesus touch me.
Let the power of the Holy Spirit fill me.
Let Your presence and grace guide, strengthen and
sustain me to reach the side of victory!

Listen...

You Are Free Indeed!

Scripture:

John 8:36 (NRSV)

So if the Son makes you free, you will be free indeed.

Message of Hope:

Decades ago, there was a game children loved to play. The call out for this game was "Olly, Olly, Oxen Free!" The German origin was "Alle, Alle, Auch Sind Frei!" The interpretation of the phrase is "Everyone, everyone also is free!" It's safe to come out of hiding! The American version of the game is Hide and Go Seek!

As I took a look at myself during the unprecedented world challenges of 2020, I noticed that I had been in hiding. Now, don't get this point twisted. I'm not referring to self-quarantine or the mandatory quarantine requested during a pandemic. We must take all measures to be safe and well.

But, as for me, I crawled up into a self-made cocoon while being at home. Oh, I got off to a great start! I participated in conference calls for work and church and fulfilled a few church duties from home. Well, that took all of two days and then I hit a wall!

There are many things I could have been doing but, I will be honest, I became extremely paranoid and fully focused on the challenges of living in the middle of COVID-19. Simply going out of the house for an afternoon walk gave me great concern. Anxiety had grabbed my spirit and caused it to tremble!

So many things can happen in life that can literally shake your spirit! Financial insecurity, chronic health issues, relationship challenges and much more can make the strongest person grow weary. When we are afraid, weary and unsure of what tomorrow will bring, we will be tempted to hide until the dust settles. We may perform our day to day responsibilities but go no further than basic survival.

Whether we are in a pandemic or some other life changing struggle, we can still be free! Because we are all God's children, we can move and breathe and pursue the dreams God has placed in our hearts. When you feel discouraged and just sick and tired of life, remember that you are a child of the Most High God! He is walking with you through every storm to give you the strength, grace, and freedom to thrive! Don't allow challenges to stunt your growth!

Prayer:

Father, Thank You for the assurance of Your presence! Whether in the storm or a season of bright days, You are always with me! Thank You for Your Son! His life, suffering, and resurrection gives all of us the freedom to be who You have designed us to be! Your love has set us free to move forward to better and brighter days! It is in the strong and matchless Name of Jesus, I pray! Amen!

Think About It:

Praise the Lord, I am free!
Free to get closer to God!
Free to explore my divine gifts and talents!
It's time to be free in the spirit to fulfill the call and the will of God!

Listen...

Serve the Lord by Serving Others

Beloved, it is God's hope that we help, equip, support, encourage and mobilize others to be the best version of themselves as they have an encounter with God. It is our divine responsibility to serve in such a way that the broken-hearted will find peace, the disadvantaged will pursue opportunity, and those who have lost hope will stand once again in the security and anticipation of God's love and presence. We can do this by meeting the needs of others through selfless giving of our time, talent, and divine resources. As needs are met, others will get a glimpse of Jesus! Souls can be won for Jesus and the Kingdom will expand by the spirit of our service!

Service: A Way of Giving Thanks

Scripture:

1 Samuel 12:24 (NRSV)

Only fear the Lord, and serve him faithfully with all your heart; for consider what great things he has done for you.

Message of Hope:

In Samuel's farewell speech, he encouraged the people to remember the great things God had done for them. Whenever a calamity arose, serving other gods and people seemed to be the best way out of a bad situation at that time. In spite of their choices, God was merciful and forgiving. It was Samuel's final hope that remembering the forgiveness, mercy, and kindness of God would be the compelling force for serving God with a thankful heart.

Have you ever made choices based on the easiest way out of a bad situation? Perhaps you knew it was a bad decision, but something had to be done! Regardless of your actions and choices, God delivered you from the total destruction your soul and life could have experienced.

If you are enjoying a delivered and set free life, the best way to say "Thank You" to God is to serve His people. Serve honestly, with all your heart. The work can get dirty, take up some of your time, and you may get tired. Giving up a portion of your time, energy, and other resources to lighten someone else's burdens is worth every moment.

Prayer:

Father, I Thank You for your divine providence over my life. Through every trial along my journey, You have protected and delivered me. So many consequences could have led to a different end, but I am thankful Your mercy said "No!" Because of Your faithfulness and grace, I can say "Thank You" through my service to others. It is in the Mighty Name of Your Son, Jesus, I pray and serve! Amen!

Think About It:

Give thanks with a grateful Servant's heart!

Service: A Way of Worship

Scripture:

Joshua 22:5 (NRSV)

Take good care to observe the commandment and instruction that Moses the servant of the Lord commanded you, to love the Lord your God, to walk in all his ways, to keep his commandments, and to hold fast to him, and serve him with all your heart and with all your soul.

Message of Hope:

Joshua restated the message of Moses to remind the people that obedience should be based on one's love for God. It was the Israelites' spiritual responsibility to serve God with all of their heart and soul. This level of service was an expression of worship.

Sometimes, just thinking about the work involved in serving God by serving others can cause us to lose focus of the main purpose of our service. The way in which we serve demonstrates who we are in Christ. Loving God with our all of our heart and soul requires us to also love and serve the people of God. He will give us the strength and resources we need to serve effectively.

God will continually restore and replenish all that we give away. Don't let the work of the service distract you from the One to be honored through your actions.

Prayer:

Father, I worship You with every part of my being. As you strengthen me and provide for the tasks ahead, I will give of my service freely to others. May my focus always be on You. It is in the Mighty Name of Your Son, Jesus, I pray and serve! Amen!

Think About It:

Worship God with the work of your hands and the resources He places under your stewardship.

Service: Our Divine Example

Scripture:

Mark 10:45 (NRSV)

For even the Son of Man came not to be served but to serve, and to give His life a ransom for many.

Message of Hope:

So, there was this thing James and John wanted desperately from Jesus. They wanted to sit next to Jesus, on each side of Him, in His kingdom. James and John wanted the top positions! Jesus told them that they really did not understand the depth of their request. They said they would be willing to do anything necessary to obtain this place of prominence. Jesus explained real greatness is obtained by serving others.

In the world's arena, greatness is identified by titles, collegiate degrees, money and other material things. Personal achievement on the job is often recognized by the seat reserved for you at the conference table. The spotlight is given to the one who has the greatest talent or at least knows the best way to steal the spotlight. If we are to truly "make it" in this world, there has to be an easy way to arrive at the top!

In Christ's Kingdom, serving others is the way to get God's reward. The desire to be on top will actually delay our Kingdom potential. Instead of looking for our personal needs to be met, we must look for ways to meet the needs of others.

Prayer:

Father, I am praying for focus as I serve. May the motives of my service be solely to please and honor You. I know You will provide everything I need to serve and to thrive. There is no title, position or earthly thing greater than Your love! As You bless me, I will strive to bless others. It is in the Mighty Name of Your Son, Jesus, I pray and serve! Amen!

Think About It:

Titles, wealth, and things will fade away. The love of God and the work we do for Him lasts throughout eternity!

Service: Press Through the Work

Scripture:

2 Chronicles 15:7 (NRSV)

But you, take courage! Do not let your hands be weak, for your work shall be rewarded.

Message of Hope:

In 2 Chronicles, chapter 15, Azariah encouraged all the men of Judah and Benjamin to keep up the good work of worshipping and serving God because their work would be rewarded. In verses 2 – 6, Azariah advised that it would be best to seek the Lord and call on Him in distress. God would be faithful to protect, deliver and reward all who trust in Him.

Recognition and rewards are great incentives on two levels. Living and serving by God's standards can bring a sense of satisfaction to our spirit. Our permanent recognition and reward will be obtained in eternity. Our work on earth may not get recognized on the local or national news. We may never see our name in the spotlight for the work we do in serving individuals or communities. Do not be weary in well doing and do not be discouraged if no one says "job well done." The best rewards are not the temporary ones. Our greatest reward will come through the blessings of God while we are here on earth and the gift of eternal life with Him.

Prayer:

Father, I pray that my service is acceptable in Your sight. May I serve for Your glory and not my own. Whether I receive earthly recognition or not, I give my service to others as an offering to Your kingdom. It is in the Mighty Name of Your Son, Jesus, I pray! Amen!

Think About It:

May the work I do and the service I give speak for me as a Beloved Child of God!

Service: Using Divine Resources

Scripture:

1 Peter 4:10 (NRSV)

Like good stewards of the manifold grace of God, serve one another with whatever gift each of you has received.

Message of Hope:

Some of us believe we can use our abilities as we please. Others believe they do not have any skills or talents to use for serving God's people. All of us have been blessed with gifts to be used for God's glory. Our abilities, knowledge and skills must be used in serving others. The gifts placed upon us are not given solely for our enjoyment. When we use our gifts to help others, they will actually see Jesus in us and be drawn to the spirit of compassion we display.

If others chose to promote their own glory and keep their gifts to themselves, we would not have inventions, electricity, airplanes, medicine, food and many other necessities and pleasures of life. As a result of many scientists and entrepreneurs, we are enjoying health, safety, fashion and a multitude of social advantages. We must be thankful to God for those who recognized and fulfilled the responsibility to bless others with their knowledge and talents.

Prayer:

Father, Thank You for the talents and skills you have placed in me! Through these gifts, I desire to be a blessing to others. May the use of all You have given me help to shine the light of Jesus to the world! It is my hope and prayer that others will be drawn to You as I serve. It is in the Mighty Name of Your Son, Jesus, I pray and serve! Amen!

Think About It:

Daily, I benefit from the gifts of others. May I use my gifts to God's glory!

Service: Tools for Our Kingdom Responsibility

Scripture:

Romans 12:10-13 (NRSV)

10 ....love one another with mutual affection; outdo one another in showing honor.
11 Do not lag in zeal, be ardent in spirit, serve the Lord.
12 Rejoice in hope, be patient in suffering, persevere in prayer.
13 Contribute to the needs of the saints; extend hospitality to strangers.

Message of Hope:

There are many ways we can honor others. Some of us honor others for what we can get from them. Some of us honor others out of expected duty. Some of us honor others to obtain a place of influence. It is God's desire that we honor each other in love with no ulterior motive.

As Christians, we should honor others because they have been created in God's image. They are our brothers and sisters in Christ and they possess gifts from our Heavenly Father. We must serve with Christian hospitality. In other words, serve with a smile on your face and love in your heart. The presentation of your service also displays the condition of your spirit. Serve by praying for those in need and ask for God's guidance as you give. Kingdom hospitality abounds when we serve in the hope of meeting the need and with a patient and kind attitude.

Prayer:

Father, I pray that my service to others displays Your loving kindness. When I feel tired, please restore my strength. When I feel challenged by the needs of others, please help me to be patient. When I don't feel like serving, please help me to remember all you have done for me! It is in the Mighty Name of Your Son, Jesus, I pray and serve! Amen!

Think About It:

When I give the best of my service, God's best shines through me!

Service: Be Willing and Be Blessed

Scripture:

1 Peter 5:2-4 (NRSV)

2 ...to tend to the flock of God that is in your charge, exercising the oversight, not under compulsion but willingly, as God would have you do it--not for sordid gain but eagerly.
3 Do not lord it over those in your charge, but be examples to the flock.
4 And when the chief shepherd appears, you will win the crown of glory that never fades away.

Message of Hope:

In this chapter of Peter's letter, he describes the characteristics of good leaders who are also servants of God. Effective servant-leaders must recognize that the people under their care belong to God. Servant leadership is accomplished through a sincere eagerness to do the work. The task is approached by the desire to give rather than to receive. When we function in these characteristics, we lead and serve God's way. The "Chief Shepherd" Peter mentions is Jesus Christ. He will reward our service and leadership when He judges all of us upon His return.

All of us should strive to serve and lead the godly way. Our young and older servant-leaders can learn from each other and work together in service. The work of service is not to be used to look down on anyone. However, God uses us to be a blessing. Our service should always result in helping another person to rise above their circumstances to become effective and fruitful workers in the vineyard of the Christian life.

Prayer:

Father, I pray that my service reflects the work of a good shepherd. May I never forget how far You have brought me and all of the mighty things You have done with my life. I pray that I see Your handiwork in every person I meet. This will help me to realize we are all creations of God to be respected and loved. I vow to be a servant who seeks to please You and give You glory! It is in the Mighty Name of Your Son, Jesus, I pray and serve! Amen!

Think About It:

Serve as a shepherd. Be willing to do the work and do not leave anyone behind!

Listen...

Always Becoming More

Scripture:

Genesis 42: 7-8 (NRSV)

7 When Joseph saw his brothers, he recognized them, but he treated them like strangers and spoke harshly to them. "Where do you come from?" he said, "From the land of Canaan, to buy food."
8 Although Joseph had recognized his brothers, they did not recognize him.

Message of Hope:

Life is a journey and a lesson in becoming more. A dear friend once told me we are always becoming. If we are sincerely seeking our destiny, we will grow from season to season and step by step. Strive to become the best version of yourself by digging deep into your mind, heart, and spirit to discover the gift of God inside of you and then use all of it for God's glory!

The becoming process is a challenge. It will not be a journey full of fun and games. You may have to release yourself from some folks and some habits. There will be times you will not like the real person you see in the mirror. Some people will not like you because you are changing for the better right before their eyes. You are breaking out of the box they had for you. You are not staying under their control.

Joseph is one of those people who sought to become more. You can find major highlights of Joseph's journey to destiny in Genesis, Chapters 39-45. Joseph endured many challenges, beginning with being a subject of taunting among his brothers. He endured physical abuse, slavery, false accusations, and was thrown in jail. But God was always present to help Joseph through his struggles because God had a plan for his life. As Joseph attained social power, he also became a vital resource for his family.

God can take you from the lowest place in life and use your pain and despair for His Glory! That's a Hallelujah moment right there! God can expand your ability to bless others. On your journey to becoming more, you will never look like what you've been through! Get ready! Those who thought they knew you may not recognize you!

Prayer:

God, I Thank You for making ways for me to become more than I ever imagined! Thank you for Your presence, protection, and favor! I am becoming more through the power and the lessons of my journey! It is in the powerful and supportive Name of Jesus, I pray! Amen!

Think About It:

Becoming all that God intended is the pursuit of His divine plan!

Listen...

Faith to Walk on Water

Scripture:

Matthew 14:28-30 (NRSV)

28 Peter answered him, "Lord, if it is you, command me to come to you on the water."
29 He said, "Come." So Peter got out of the boat, started walking on the water, and came toward Jesus.
30 But when he noticed the strong wind, he became frightened, and beginning to sink, he cried out, "Lord, save me!"

Message of Hope:

Problems, challenges, disappointments and other hardships of life can seem like an out-of-control storm. The issues of today's society can tempt us to give up hope. Situations can change so quickly. In the blink of an eye, your entire life can be turned upside down, disturbing the vessel holding your ambitions and dreams.

The disciples also had times filled with despair and moments when doubt tossed them around the boat! Well, doubt is a very real tool the enemy uses to distract us from the possibilities of God. To arrive at our divine purpose, we must shift from doubt to walking-on-water faith.

Like the disciples, many of us have seen God move in unimaginable ways. He has a track record for performing the miraculous in our lives. Your current storms, however, may cause doubt to tiptoe around your soul. Remember the blessings of yesterday and listen for God to speak a way of deliverance today. If you begin to doubt, look up to the heavens and cry out "Lord, help me!"

Prayer:

Father, you have been so faithful. When my doubts and fears arise, I will look to You. When my strength is weakened and my blessed assurance is frail, Lord, I will cry unto You! In the Strong Name of Jesus, I pray! Amen!

Think About It:

Trust God and His divine power!
You can push through the storm with walking-on-water faith!

Listen...

You Are a Difference Maker!

Genesis 7:1 (NRSV)

Then the Lord said to Noah, "Go into the ark, you and all your household, for I have seen that you alone are righteous before me in this generation.

Message of Hope:

Beloved, we were created, anointed, gifted, and given divine purpose to become Difference Makers! We are designed to make a positive impact in the lives of others. Difference Makers are inventors, mentors, counselors, teachers, comforters and all who usher us toward healing and hope in the pursuit of our destiny.

As I thought about this clarion call from God for us to become Difference Makers, Noah came to mind. God considered Noah righteous and blameless because Noah wholeheartedly loved and obeyed God. Noah spent his life walking step by step in faith.

God assigned Noah to build an ark on dry land. Noah had to exercise a huge degree of obedience and he had to be devoted to a long-term commitment. Some Theologians believe the ark took approximately 120 years to build in a region that had not seen rain in a very long time. Noah's obedience led to God's protection and a future for his family and all creatures sheltering in the ark.

The only long-term commitment Noah's job can be slightly compared to is our own lives. We can wisely spend our lifetime committed to accepting God's grace through obedience and gratitude! That in itself would be a lifetime project well managed!

God is asking you to be a Difference Maker! Remain available to the will of God for your life. Listen for God's instructions. He speaks in various ways. Then, follow His instructions carefully. Agree to be a Difference Maker and God will protect, provide, and prosper you and everyone connected to you!

Prayer:

Father, Thank You for equipping me to make a difference. I give my heart, soul, and mind to you to design my divine assignment. I pray for the energy, obedience, and focus to do Your will and become a blessing to others. In the Strong Name of Jesus, I trust and pray! Amen!

Think About It:

Let's make a difference!
One person, following the call of God can be a Difference Maker!
I am a Difference Maker and I matter in God's Kingdom!

Listen...

Treasure the Time

Scripture:

Esther 4:16 (NRSV)

"Go, gather all the Jews to be found in Susa, and hold a fast on my behalf, and neither eat nor drink for three days, night or day. I and my maids will also fast as you do. After that I will go to the king, though it is against the law; and if I perish, I perish."

Message of Hope:

Time is a treasure more valuable than any jewel or the largest bank account. There is no rebate on time. Once you have used a specific point in time, it's gone forever. During the years of Queen Esther's life, there were vigorous attempts made to eliminate the Jewish community. Their time on earth was sought to be wiped out! But God sovereignly preserved His people as He said He would in His covenant promise to Abraham.

Queen, Esther found herself in a position of great influence at a most crucial time. She decided to use the time and position entrusted to her to be a blessing to her people. Esther answered God's call, followed His plan, and made the most of her appointed time.

Beloved, treasure the time God has given you. Answer the call of God on your life. Use the connections, education, skills and resources you have to be a blessing to others. Seek the Lord so that you may take action and treasure your appointed time.

Prayer:

Father, Thank You for allowing me to be present in this time in history! Thank You for trusting me to make the best use of my time, talents and gifts you placed in me to bless others. It is my prayer that I don't waste time, but treasure each day You give me. Thank You for the precious gift of life! It is in the Unparalleled Name of Jesus, I pray!

Think About It:

God has great opportunities for you to do His work!
Time is of the essence!

Listen...

Pressing Through the Tunnel

Scripture:

Philippians 3:13-14 (NRSV)

13 Beloved, I do not consider that I have made it my own; but this one thing I do: forgetting what lies behind and straining forward to what lies ahead,
14 I press on toward the goal for the prize of the heavenly call of God in Christ Jesus.

Message of Hope:

The challenges of COVID-19 certainly resembled the confinement felt when we travel through tunnels. Like tunnels, a pandemic is a season of restrictions. I don't recall ever hearing anyone say they like tunnels. The tunnel of love may be an exception! Some people describe the effects of tunnels as hypnotic or claustrophobic. There is no official term for a fear of tunnels, but it is often diagnosed as agoraphobia, where a person perceives the environment as being difficult to escape.

We use tunnels to get from one point to another because tunnels shorten the distance of the journey and help us cross over mountains, go around hills, or go through water. The journey of life can present a lot of tunnels that we may not like, but they all lead to our destiny. Oftentimes, we can get stuck in the tunnels along the journey. But, tunnels are a passageway. We are not supposed to set up camp in the tunnel. Every tunnel has an entry and an exit.

Our mistakes, regrets, disappointments and failures can cause us to get stuck in the tunnel of our past. But, if you release those heavy weights of the past as you keep pressing your way through the tunnel, you will find evidence that you are reaching the exit. The promises of God, new opportunities, growth in your faith and prayer life are God's rays of hope waiting at the end of the tunnel.

Prayer:

Thank You God for the power and grace to press onward. As I move ahead, I vow to shake off the weight of my past. God, I look forward to seeing that divine light at the end of my tunnel! In the Strong Name of Jesus, I pray! Amen!

Think About It:

Victory, power, strength, grace, wisdom, goodness and healing are waiting at the exit of my tunnel!
I am pressing toward the light...the prize of God!

Listen...

Are You Ready?

Scripture:

Matthew 25:7-9 (NRSV)

7 Then all those bridesmaids got up and trimmed their lamps.
8 The foolish said to the wise, 'Give us some of your oil, for our lamps are going out.'
9 But the wise replied, 'No! there will not be enough for you and for us; you had better go to the dealers and buy some for yourselves.'

Message of Hope:

The Parable of the Ten Bridesmaids is found in Matthew 25:1-13. I encourage you to read the entire parable. Their story shows us the benefits of being ready for opportunity and the consequences of opportunity catching you by surprise.

All of the Bridesmaids wanted to meet the Bridegroom, but all of them were not ready! Perhaps the five foolish Bridesmaids were excited, eager and anxious but they didn't properly prepare for the Bridegroom. The excitement of meeting Him distracted them from the blessing they so greatly desired.

Many of us may believe we are ready for the blessings we dream of and pray for daily, but our anticipation could cause us to be unprepared. Drop the excitement and anxious attractions to prepare for the day opportunity knocks!

Don't forget your oil! You have it! Prepare it! Nurture it! The oil is your anointing and covering from God. All of the gifts in you will prepare you for your destiny. You never know when or how your Kingdom opportunity is going to drop into your life. It will be so much better for you to be ready and not caught by surprise!

Prayer:

Father, I want to be ready when You manifest divine opportunities. I pray that I stay attentive to the move of Your hand in my life. Thank You for the plans you have destined to come my way! In the Strong Name of Jesus, I pray! Amen!

Think About It:

Don't be caught by surprise!
Nurture your gifts!
Don't fall asleep!
Be prepared for your Kingdom Opportunity!

Listen...

Start Salting Your Purpose

Scripture:

Ezekiel 16:4 (NRSV)

As for your birth, on the day you were born your navel cord was not cut, nor were you washed with water to cleanse you, nor rubbed with salt, nor wrapped in cloths.

Matthew 5:13 (NRSV)

You are the salt of the earth; but if salt has lost its taste, how can its saltiness be restored? It is no longer good for anything, but it is thrown out and trampled under foot.

Message of Hope:

Salt was an important mineral in the ancient world and remains as such today. In the appropriate amounts, salt is important for good health as a seasoning and to purify and preserve certain foods and commodities.

In Biblical days, God and the people of God made covenants of salt which implied faithfulness, dependability and durability of relationships. The Israelites rubbed their newborn babies with salt to keep them free from diseases and other infections.

Matthew 5:13 describes God's children as the salt that heals and preserves others. We must preserve our salt, our gifts and talents, with the power of a relationship with God. Following every whim and false doctrine will add poison to the salt you have been given to bless the earth.

Perhaps someone forgot to rub you with salt in your early years. Someone forgot to rub you with the salt of encouragement and positive support. So many of us have gifts and talents we are hiding under a rock because stepping out on faith wouldn't seem logical!

The salt of the covenant promise made by God to always be with us will preserve our purpose and heal the wounds of the past. We have everything we need to be the salt of the earth! Amp up your prayer life! Seek the will of God for your life! Let your gifts and talents shine in everything you do! Do the work to add power to your salt!

Prayer:

Father, I am thankful that my salt is still available. Becoming the salt of the earth is in my divine DNA. I vow to consider the way I talk, give attention to my relationship with You, and give my very best to others. In the Strong Name of Jesus, I pray! Amen!

Think About It:

Do not neglect your saltiness!
Add divine, flavorful blessings to the lives of others!

Listen...

Accept God's Reboot

Scripture:

2 Corinthians 12:8-10 (NRSV)

8 Three times I appealed to the Lord about this, that it would leave me, 9 but he said to me, "My grace is sufficient for you, for power is made perfect in weakness." So, I will boast all the more gladly of my weaknesses, so that the power of Christ may dwell in me.
10 Therefore I am content with weaknesses, insults, hardships, persecutions, and calamities for the sake of Christ; for whenever I am weak, then I am strong.

Message of Hope:

The challenges of life can result in a weary soul, tired body and the loss of hope. Trials and tribulations can weaken and distract us. Disappointments and betrayal can cause us to lose heart. Whatever happens along life's journey, we can connect to God's reboot of grace.

Scripture doesn't reveal the thorn in Paul's flesh, but we know it was an irritation and he repeatedly asked God to remove it. Some theologians suggest Paul had malaria, or epilepsy. Whatever it was, we can imagine it must have been debilitating. The thorn reminded Paul that he had to be in constant contact with God.

God didn't remove this challenge, but Paul kept moving even when he was weak. He demonstrates how the grace of God can give you a reboot to strengthen you in the middle of your journey when challenges and pain will not go away. The middle is not a time to sit back and wallow in our calamity. The middle of the challenge is a time to reach out to God in prayer and get as close to Him as possible. Strengthen your relationship with God and be empowered by His amazing grace!

Prayer:

Father, Thank You for Your Grace! When times get rough and I get tired, I know I can run to You and be recharged! Your Grace is more than enough to strengthen me along this journey of life! It is in the Strong Name of Jesus, I pray! Amen!

Think About It:

When you grow weary and dismayed, let God give you a divine reboot! With His grace, you can face anything!

Listen...

Shoulders

Scripture:

Exodus 17:11-12 (NRSV)

11 Whenever Moses held up his hand, Israel prevailed; and whenever he lowered his hand, Amalek prevailed.
12 But Moses' hands grew weary; so they took a stone and put it under him, and he sat on it. Aaron and Hur held up his hands, one on one side, and the other on the other side; so his hands were steady until the sun set.

Message of Hope:

Who's shoulders do you stand on today? Have you been the shoulders someone else needed? Hopefully, there has been someone at some point in your life who encouraged you and cheered you on as you worked towards a goal. Perhaps there is someone who has been a mentor or example you have followed to reach a special achievement.

No one succeeds at anything without traveling the path created by those who came before them. More than 50 women have had the desire to occupy the highest office of President of the United States. It doesn't matter that they didn't win. It is noteworthy to recognize they created the shoulders for others to stand upon in the pursuit of public office. There are many people throughout your blood line and beyond who have taken on challenges and accomplished great things to clear the way for your destiny and became shoulders of support.

In the scripture noted, we see what can happen when we step up and support each other. The Amalekites were a fierce tribe. Aaron and Hur could see Moses was getting tired and they stood beside Moses to hold up his arms, encouraging their army to victory.

Let's set the example for others. We can pave the way for the destiny of many. Someone, perhaps a stranger to you, made a way for you. It's time to be the shoulders of support for others.

Prayer:

God, Thank You for everyone you placed in my life to be the shoulders I need. I give You Glory for the shoulders of Your Son that carried my sins to the cross. Give me the strength each day to support someone else along life's journey. It is in the Strong Name of Jesus, I pray! Amen!

Think About It:

When we Encourage, Support and Strengthen each other, we make the future a brighter place!

Listen...

Disappointments Happen

Scripture:

2 Corinthians 4:7-9

7 But we have this treasure in clay jars, so that it may be made clear that this extraordinary power belongs to God and does not come from us.
8 We are afflicted in every way, but not crushed; perplexed, but not driven to despair;
9 Persecuted, but not forsaken; struck down, but not destroyed;

Romans 8:18

I consider that the sufferings of this present time are not worth comparing with the glory about to be revealed in us.

Message of Hope:

If you have never been disappointed, I would love to meet you because you are one rare individual! We cannot journey through this life without some disappointments. Untruths, broken promises, and heartbreak will visit all of us. Sometimes, disappointments are unintentional and at other times they are orchestrated with the offender's benefit in mind.

Your disappointment is not the end. It will not utterly destroy you. Instead, disappointments are opportunities to grow your character and gift of discernment. As you move toward forgiveness, you will learn who you can trust and who you need to place on guard. As you mature through your disappointing times, the opportunity to pray for yourself and the person who disappointed you will encourage your soul.

A disappointment is an opportunity for God to do His best work in us. Once you come out of the heartache, betrayal and despair, you will be stronger! You will not be so easily taken in the next time deception presents itself. Those past painful experiences will have taught you well and your gift of discernment will function at a higher level. So, learn from the hurt and allow yourself to grow through the pain.

Prayer:

Father, disappointments are sometimes a heavy burden. I pray for strength, grace and mercy to endure knowing that You are right beside me! Thank You for Your love! Thank You for picking me up every time disappointment knocks me down! In Jesus' Name, I pray and my soul is grateful! Amen!

Think About It

God forgives and forgets when I repeatedly disappoint Him.
Father, teach me to express Your example of forgiveness toward others.

Listen...

Follow the Leader

Scripture:

Proverbs 3:6

In all your ways acknowledge him, and he will make straight your paths.

Psalm 23:2-3

2 He makes me lie down in green pastures;
3 he restores my soul. He leads me in right paths for his name's sake.

Message of Hope:

While vacationing in Ottawa, Canada many years ago, I decided I would attend a local church for Sunday morning worship. I was not familiar with the area and had no information about the churches in town. Determined to uphold my commitment to worship, I began walking in the community to find a church.

There were several churches available, but I wasn't sure of the one for me. As I walked, I prayed that God would lead me to the church where I would be blessed. There was a Catholic Church and a Baptist Church along my path but I did not feel led to go into either church. As I approached Bethel Pentecostal Church, I knew it was the church for me to visit. The service was awesome and I felt right at home!

I had allowed myself to be led by God and experienced the realization of the guidance found in prayer. When we fully submit to God's lead, we will not slip along the way. God will order our steps and decisions to get us to the destination He has ordained. When we arrive at that right place along the straight paths, we will find joy, peace, calmness of spirit and restoration for our weary, wondering souls.

Prayer:

God, Thank You for divine direction. I pray that I look to You when I'm lost during the challenges of life and decision-making seasons. You know me better than I even think I know myself. Your guidance I will seek. Your wisdom I will apply. In the Strong Name of Jesus, I trust and pray!

Think About It:

Allow God to be your compass
Find direction in His word
Seek His will in prayer
Don't look to others, Look to God...He knows the perfect way

Listen...

Identity Crisis

Scriptures:

Psalm 37:4

Delight yourself in the Lord; and he shall give you the desires of your heart.

Psalm 100:3

It is God who has made us and not we ourselves.

Message of Hope:

Do certain things, people, or titles give you a sense of identity? Some women identify or validate themselves by their beauty. Others base their identity or self-worth on the person they marry or professional accomplishments. Some men and women feel like a real person of notice by the kind of car they drive or the size of their bank account. There are some people who thrive on having control over everything because it gives them a sense of importance. I am sure many of us know folks who live for personal attention!

Why is it necessary to use certain things or people to define who we are and give purpose to our lives? You received your identity before God placed you in your mother's womb. Instead of focusing on people and things for your identity and sense of fulfillment, seek the love of God and He will reveal your purpose and His plan for your life. True happiness and fulfillment comes from our Creator because He knows us best!

The next time you feel insignificant and only "important" when you are surrounded by things and people, remember the most important part of you is that you belong to God! You are a member of a peculiar people; a royal priesthood set aside for the purpose of glorifying God! Nothing or no one on earth can define you! Your identity comes from God!

Prayer:

Father, Thank You for calling me Your friend and Your child! As the Creator of all things, You are the designer of all people! Everything I am and everything I ever hope to be is made possible by You! Thank You for my divine identity! It is in the strong Name of Jesus, The Christ, I trust, believe, and pray! Amen!

Think About It:

I was running and You found me
I was blinded and You gave me sight
I was dying and You gave me life
Lord You are my identity
I know who I am! I know who I am!
I am Yours and You are mine!
Jesus You are Mine!

(*I Know Who I Am* - Israel Houghton and New Breed)

Listen...

A Night Season

Scripture:

Psalm 30:5 (NRSV)

For his anger is but for a moment; his favor is for a lifetime. Weeping may linger for the night, but joy comes with the morning.

Message of Hope:

This message was written during the COVID-19 pandemic. Month after month; it seemed as if the pandemic was one long and dreadful night. Staying positive and upbeat from day to day is challenging even to the most devout Christian. During this season, many people said God allowed it because He was angry with the world.

In the middle of the pandemic, racism seemed to gain a second wind and rise up stronger than ever. The distress and discussions we were having in the 1960s were revisited more than 55 years later! The U.S. was experiencing the same problems but with new faces and methods of operation.

This really does sound like a long weary night of God's anger doesn't it! The struggles of this time caused many of us to weep constantly. Well, at this writing, the pandemic is not over and the challenges of racism are still a reality. It is my prayer that all has changed for the better by the time you pick up this book! The thing to hold on to is the fact that every night, no matter how long, is followed by morning. God sees our tears and knows our pain.

When you are faced with a personal storm, hold on to the truth that the sun must follow the storm. The forces of evil will work overtime in attempts to conquer your soul. Fear and doubt will be your greatest opponents. Depression may sit awhile and demand attention from your mind and emotions. Do not give in and do not give up before the battle is won! God will hold your hand through the night, if you let Him. He will wipes all tears away and give you peace in the middle of the night and hope for that better day...morning!

Prayer:

Father, when night time falls in my life, I pray for strength and grace to hold on to You. I pray I can resist the urge to allow the distractions of pain and despair to cause me to wander from You. I pray for grace to hold on to the truth! You see my tears and hear my plea! In the strong and loving Name of Jesus, I trust and pray! Amen!

Think About It:

When my night seems so very long and my faith grows weak, Precious Lord, linger near. Take my hand and guide me through until my soul can envision a new day!

Listen...

Don't Play It Safe

Scripture:

Romans 8:35-37 (NRSV)

35 Who will separate us from the love of Christ? Will hardship, or distress, or persecution, or famine, or nakedness, or peril, or sword?
36 As it is written, "For your sake we are being killed all day long; we are accounted as sheep to be slaughtered."
37 No, in all these things we are more than conquerors through him who loved us.

Message of Hope:

Some people like limitations, whether real or self-imposed, because limitations can provide a sense of safety. That feeling of being safe and protected by so-called limitations is a lie from the pit of hell where demonic control rules. It's not safe in there! There are no true friends, no support, no strength and no growth in fake limitations! We will have to break free from those limitations to answer the command, "don't play it safe!"

Some people and things become dominant over us as long as we let them have control. People, habits, and the challenges of life can keep us "in our place" if we let them. You know...that place where we allow people and things to define us...that so called place where you belong. Playing it safe blocks us from arriving at our divine identity.

May I encourage you to take a leap of faith? Don't Play It Safe! Discover what God called you to do. Reject the notion to stay in that lane someone else determined for you. Push back the fear of having to put in some work to pursue your destiny. Turn off the volume of what they say and what they think. Who are "they?" Anyone who has an opinion of who they think you should be is not in tune with God's desires for your life.

Recognize God's role in your identity. Pursue your destiny knowing anything that tries to block you cannot separate you from God's love. God really does work through every circumstance in your life to bring you to a good end. No obstacle that comes your way can block His plan.

Prayer:

God, Thank You for protecting me and preserving my place in Your heart. I can move forward and I don't have to play it safe. You are my refuge. No matter what comes my way, I am more than a conqueror because I am Your Beloved! It is in the Name of Your Only Beloved Son, Jesus, I pray! Amen!

Think About It:

When we don't play it safe, we allow God to clear the path to our future!

We win redemption!
We win favor with God!
We win eternal life!